BOB LOVES SALMON

Including the legend of

Salmon Woman
and her
Children

Written and Illustrated by

N. Scrantz Lersch

Copyright 2016 by N. Scrantz Lersch

All rights reserved, including the right to reproduce this book or portions thereof in any form whatsoever.

For permission contact:

Scrantz

Studio 37
Portland, Oregon
Madison, Wisconsin
USA
at
scrantz@gmail.com

Bob Loves Salmon
1. Salmon Biology 2. Salmon Legend 3. Pacific Northwest
4. Oncoryhnchus 5. Salmon Life Cycle 6. Salmon Anatomy 7. Fish
8. Marine Biology 9. Native American Legend 10. Salmon Recipe
11. Rainbow Trout 12. Cutthroat Trout 13. Salmo
14. Kokanee 15. Limnology 16. Bob Loves to Learn Series

Studio 37 Publications
3737 NE Alameda Street
Portland, Oregon 97212

ISBN-13: 978-1535150026
ISBN-10: 1535150025

For Russell and Harrison

Dedicated to all those who
take children to the library
and outside to play.

Bob woke up every morning and looked out his window.

He was very curious.

Bob loved to learn new things.

Bob and his friends, Michelle, Javier, Julie, Eddie, Rosa and Jack, wanted to learn everything about SALMON.

Salmon are amazing, silvery FISH that live in the ocean. They can swim for hundreds of miles.

Bob learned that salmon live in both the Pacific and the Atlantic Ocean.

Salmon travel in large groups to avoid being eaten by orca whales and sea lions.

A large group of salmon is called a SCHOOL of fish.

Salmon eat krill and small fish, like herring and anchovies.

What lives in the ocean but is NOT BORN in the ocean?

SALMON!

Adult salmon live in the ocean for two to eight years. Then they migrate from the ocean to the river or stream where they were born.

Their bodies change when they move from salt water to fresh water.

Some salmon swim for a thousand miles UPRIVER and jump many waterfalls to reach their birth river.

Salmon are ANADROMOUS*.

*ANADROMOUS - from Greek: ana = UP, dromos = RUNNING

When the salmon reach their birthplace they are ready to SPAWN.
To SPAWN means to lay eggs.

Bob learned that FEMALE SALMON lay their eggs in a gravel nest called a REDD.

A female makes a redd by turning on her side and beating her tail in the gravel.

MALE SALMON deposit their milt over the eggs.

The salmon eggs hatch after about two months. Michelle discovered that baby salmon are called ALEVINS.

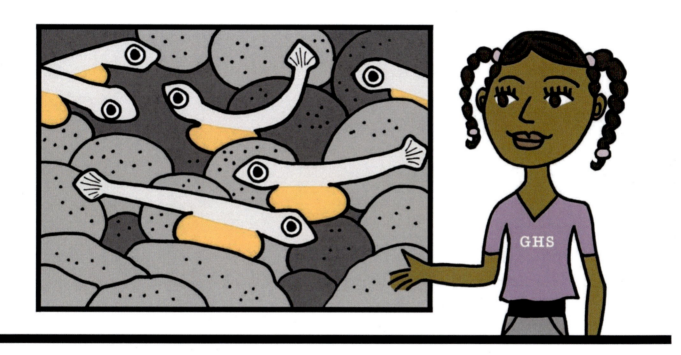

The alevins hide in the gravel and grow for about three weeks.

Alevins are about one inch long.

When these small fish grow big enough
to eat tiny plants and water insects
they are called SALMON FRY.

Javier learned that salmon fry have
stripes called PARR MARKS.
These stripes and spots help the young fish
hide in the river from PREDATORS.

A PREDATOR is an animal that eats other animals.

After several months the young salmon are ready to migrate to the ocean. These salmon are called SMOLTS.

Eddie discovered that they swim downriver to the ESTUARY where the salt water of the ocean mixes with the fresh water of the river.

Their bodies change to be able to live in the salt water and the smolts become silvery like adult salmon.

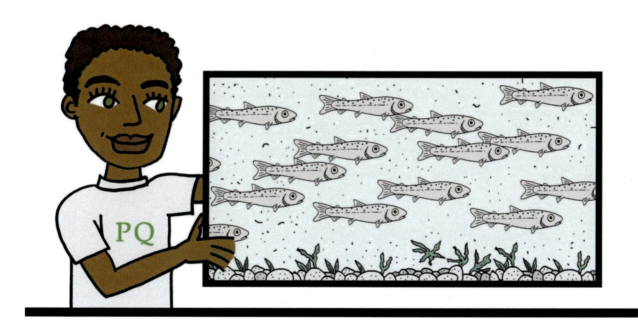

Finally, the young salmon swim into the ocean where they live and grow for several years before returning to their birth river to spawn.

What animal has NO HANDS
and NO FEET but
can CLIMB LADDERS?

SALMON!

Salmon can "climb"
FISH LADDERS.

A fish ladder
does NOT
look like this!

A fish ladder is a set of man-made small step waterfalls that migratory salmon use to travel around dams.

Grandma Shen explained that fish ladders are built next to the dams that block rivers so salmon can swim around them.

Salmon swim by moving their
FINS back and forth.
Salmon have 8 fins.

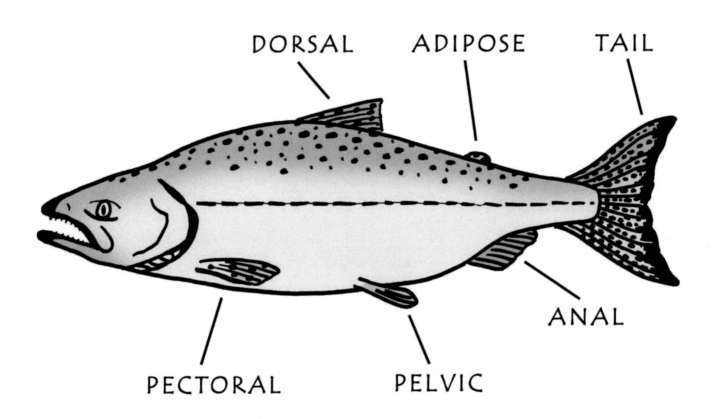

One dorsal fin, one adipose fin, one tail fin,
one anal fin, two pectoral fins and two pelvic fins.

Jack learned that SALMON have TEETH!

They use their sharp, needlelike teeth to grab their prey.

Salmon do not chew their food.

Salmon have black or gray tongues!

Rosa discovered that SALMON skin does not have HAIR.

Salmon skin has overlapping SCALES. These grow as the fish grows and have RINGS.

You can count the rings to find the age of the salmon!

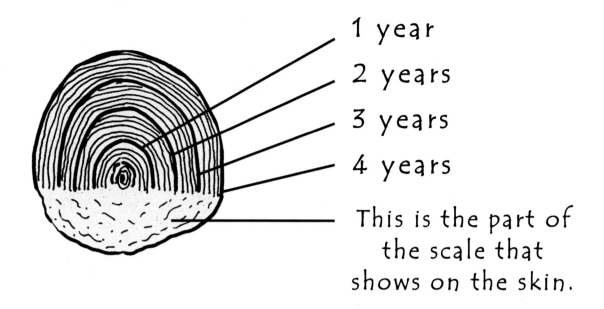

1 year
2 years
3 years
4 years

This is the part of the scale that shows on the skin.

Rosa learned that the First Peoples of the Arctic made boots and coats from salmon skin.

Salmon skin boots are WATERPROOF!

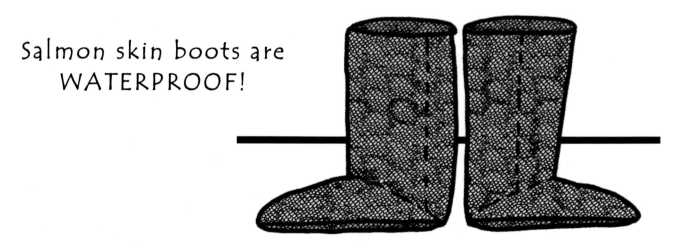

Michelle found that there are many kinds of SALMON living in the oceans.

Her friend, Javier, showed her a trick to remember the most common types of Pacific Ocean SALMON.

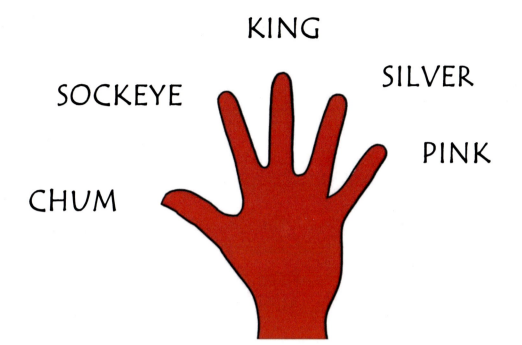

SOCKEYE KING SILVER PINK CHUM

Thumb = CHUM Salmon

Pointer = SOCKEYE Salmon

Tall Man = KING Salmon

Ring Man = SILVER Salmon

Pinky = PINK Salmon

KING salmon are also called CHINOOK salmon.
They can grow to be the biggest salmon.

Eddie found that the largest CHINOOK salmon can be over 80 pounds and almost 5 feet long!

CHINOOK salmon have spots on their backs and on their tail fins.

CHUM salmon are also called
KETA or dog salmon.

SOCKEYE salmon are also called RED salmon.

Julie learned that the word "sockeye" comes from a Native American word, "sukkai", which means fish.

SILVER salmon are also called
COHO salmon or SILVERS.

PINK salmon are also called
HUMPBACK salmon or HUMPIES.
Pink salmon are the smallest salmon.

Charley the cat discovered that every
animal has a scientific name.
Salmon are in the SALMONIDAE Family.

Pacific Salmon are in the GENUS
ONCORHYNCHUS (on-ko-RINK-us).
Each type has a different SPECIES name.

KING (Chinook) Salmon = Oncorhynchus tshawytsha
SOCKEYE = Oncorhynchus nerka
SILVER (Coho) = Oncorhynchus kisutch
CHUM (Keta) = Oncorhynchus keta
PINK = Oncorhynchus gorbuscha

Atlantic Salmon are in the
Genus SALMO.
They are called Salmo salar.

I am Felis catus

Some sockeye salmon have adapted to stay in fresh water for their entire lives.
These fish are known as KOKANEE.
(KO-kan-ee)
Kokanee live far from the ocean in lakes and creeks.

Bob learned that TROUT are also in the GENUS Oncorhynchus.

CUTTHROAT Trout = Oncorhynchus clarkii

RAINBOW Trout = Oncorhynchus mykiss

Some rainbow trout migrate to the ocean and return to their birth rivers to spawn. These fish are known as STEELHEAD trout.

Jack and Rosa discovered that
Native American people had a LEGEND, a story,
about why SALMON return to the rivers.

A LEGEND is a traditional story passed down
from generation to generation.

Salmon Woman
and her
Children

Many years ago when the world was young, the First People lived by a great river and traveled throughout their territory to find food to eat. They were led by Raven, who took them to the mountains to hunt and into the woods to gather berries and roots. One year they could not find enough to eat and Raven knew he must find another source of food or his people would starve.

Raven had never explored the great ocean before, but he knew he must try. His canoe was brought to the river's edge. He gathered his cedar bark hat, his tule mat and his canoe paddle. The people came to the shore and sang songs for him wishing him strength and luck for his journey. Raven climbed into his canoe, set out across the water and did not look back. He did not want his people to know he was afraid.

Raven paddled and searched and went farther than he had ever gone before. Many days and nights passed and still he found no food for his people. He lay in his canoe and began to cry, "I cannot find food for my people and I fear they may starve!"

Far off in the distant waters Salmon Woman heard Raven's song. She heard his crying and listened to his sadness. She felt badly for him and wanted to help. She swam up near his canoe and yelled, "Hey! Hey!"

Raven sat up and paddled towards the voice thinking that someone had fallen out of another canoe. He saw her, took her hand, pulled her into his canoe and wrapped her in his blanket. Raven gave her the last of his food and water.

He waited while she rested and then told the story of his people and how he could not find food for them

Salmon Woman was moved by Raven's kindness and decided to help. She said, "I am Salmon Woman and I have many children. My children play in the ocean all around you and sparkle in the sun. They come whenever I call them." Raven looked around but he could not see anyone nearby.

Salmon Woman said, "You cannot see them, they swim below the surface of the sea. I will introduce you." She asked to borrow Raven's cedar hat and began to sing a beautiful song.

As she sang, she dipped the hat and each time she came up with a Salmon child. "These are my children. This one is called Chinook. This one is called Coho. This one is called Chum. This one is called Pink. This one is called Sockeye."

Soon the water around the canoe was churning with Salmon children. Salmon Woman told Raven that she had more children than she could count but she knew each one by name and loved them all. "I give my children to you so your people can survive."

Raven thanked her and started paddling towards home.

As he paddled, Salmon Woman sang her beautiful song and the salmon children followed the canoe. Soon Raven's people heard the song across the water and ran to the shore. They saw Raven with a woman in his canoe.

Raven told the story of how Salmon Woman came to help him. He told them the water was filled with salmon children and that she would share them with the people.

Raven loved Salmon Woman and asked her to be his wife. Salmon Woman loved Raven because he cared so deeply for his people. They were married and spent many years together and were happy. The salmon children stayed nearby in the river and the people never had to worry about food.

After a time however, the people forgot to be grateful. One day a child said, "I am sick of salmon! All we have to eat is baked salmon, boiled salmon, smoked salmon, and dried salmon, every day!"

Salmon Woman heard this and was hurt. She stood by the water's edge and began to sing a new song.

She walked into the water and gathered her children around her. Then Salmon Woman swam away singing her song, taking all her children with her.

Raven was sad and upset. He called and called for her but Salmon Woman did not come home. The people became hungry and they begged him to search for her and bring her back. Finally he set off in his canoe across the great ocean to find his wife. After many days he found Salmon Woman and asked her to come back to the river.

Salmon Woman still loved Raven but she would not come to him until he promised that the people would always respect her and her children. There would be new conditions.

The salmon children would not stay near the village year round because the people took them for granted. During certain seasons, the salmon children would go upstream. At other times they would return to their home in the ocean. But every year, the salmon children would return to the river.

When Raven and his people agreed, Salmon Woman sang her song and led the salmon children back to the river.

Everyone lived happily once again. Every year they have a great celebration when the salmon children return to the river.

The End

MARINADE for SALMON
(for one pound of fish)

4 T. soy sauce
3 T. balsamic vinegar
1 T. sugar
1 T. sesame oil
½ t. chili paste
1 clove garlic minced

Mix together and marinate fish, skin side up for 30 minutes, or up to 24 hours.

Set oven to 350.

Place marinade and fish in a baking pan, skin side down.

Cover pan with foil.

Bake salmon until fish flakes easily.

Spoon marinade over fish before serving.

Bob and his friends learned that many animals depend on salmon for food. The bears, eagles and blue herons who live near the rivers rely on the salmon returning every year.

They discovered that there are scientists that study the animals and plants that live in rivers and lakes. They are called LIMNOLOGISTS.

Bob learned that there are scientists who study the oceans and the animals and plants that live in the sea. They are called MARINE BIOLOGISTS.

He thinks that HE might become a Marine Biologist someday!

DRAW A SALMON HERE!

About the Author

N. Scrantz Lersch likes to draw pictures,
read books and play outside whenever she can.
She especially loves swimming and walking in the woods.

The author has also written
Waiting for the Next Crisis - A Memoir, for adult readers.

Made in the USA
Columbia, SC
25 April 2022